STRAIGHT LINES AND
UNICORNS

JOHN KNIGHT

STRAIGHT LINES
AND
UNICORNS

LONDON

The Cresset Press

1960

For my wife and for my friends,
among whom special thanks are due
to Robin Skelton for
the utter generosity of his help
and encouragement

CONTENTS

ACKNOWLEDGMENTS

Some of these poems have appeared in *Enigma*, *The New English Weekly*, *New Poems* 1958 (*PEN*), *Outposts*, *Poetry* (Chicago), *Solem* and *The Spectator*, or have been broadcast in the BBC Third Programme. I am grateful to Mr John Hayward for the title of one poem and for comments leading to several improvements. *The Voice* began with the memory (only later recognized as such) of the line—*Wanders the proud sea-skimmer, shambles the drowned*—in the very different context of Mr John Heath-Stubbs' *Drowned Man* (*Beauty and the Beast*, Routledge, 1945); and the words are used with their rightful owner's kind consent.

Invocation

Speak, unicorn with speckled wings:
teach me your few and lucent words.

Aurora of the seven veils
snuffs out the darkness of the mind:
                    in ice, flame.

Speak, cold and silent Queen of Chess:
teach me your few and cogent words.

Mary and Martha pray and plan;
Lazarus turns within the mind:
                    in grass, bone.

Speak, lemur in the orchid tree:
teach me your few and mutant words.

Adam, who wrote the Song of Songs,
was once a cell in Lilith's mind:
                    in the rose, time.

Sing, stormcock on the topmost twig:
teach me your few and potent words.

The hosts of Merlin rise again,
wild daffodils within the mind:
                    in the tiderace, calm.

The Seventh Day

The first day was the joy of love
God was in his making
The scent of hay in fields.

The next day was the joy of waiting
God was in his carrying
Spring pushing under white hills.

The third day was the joy of birth
God was in his bearing
Candles light the willows.

The fourth day was the joy of breasts
God was in his suckling
Honey in the bees' domes.

The fifth day was the joy of finding
God was in his chuckling
Laughter at the brook's source.

The sixth day was the joy of words
God was in his speaking
Bluebells answer the beech.

The seventh day was the day the bombers came.

Snow

Grey is the afternoon,
    the racked seas groan,
the snarling breeze embitters
    that leviathan.

The myriad light,
    inflected shade,
the six-rayed waters,
    gather like hate.

After the strange threat,
    the refracted doubt,
the flood's flaked laughter
    on the desolate heart.

Shadow

We walked down and down to the long sea loch
past the empty inn to the house at the landing place.
Boatman and enemy sea were calm, grimly against the sun,
his vast shadow cast on the slow flow of relentless water.

      Where, we asked, shall we find Mrs McLeod?
             Not here.
      Does she not live on this side of the ferry?
             She does not.

      When the boatman had rowed us over the loch
             We asked again
      At what house does Mrs McLeod live?
             At none here.

      Where must we go, then, to find Mrs McLeod?
             I cannot say.
      And yet we were told last night that she welcomed strangers.
             She used to. Not now.

We walked up and up from the sombre beautiful loch
past the crouching kirk and the croft where Mrs McLeod
was welcome, brought by a boatman as tall as the vast shadow
he cast on the fast flow of relentless years.

All Souls

for Robin Skelton

We will leave unlocked the door
lay bread, wine, bed
build up the fire

in case some unborn pair
or, it may be, dead
should visit this house tonight

out of the obscure air
eat the today of bread
drink the tonight of wine

and before dawn quietly clear
the table and make the bed
and put a blessing on life

and put a blessing on life, and on love, and on death.

A Wind in Winter

for Rina

Along the cloudburst of the dry and blizzard stanza
stalactites of Winter go sowing the Sahara,

along the downdraught of the moon and torrent image
cascades of Spring come planting out the whirlpool,

among the squirrel branches of the sky and leafy poem
the strings and woodwind cast the keys of Summer,

and slow, fast, the long green waves break blue.

Three Faces

Green as bottle
clear as thin air
the running stillness
of crosshatched water
unknows the land,

blue as eyebright
sky and cloudy
the lace and ferment
of snowdrift water
loveplays with land,

kaleidoscopic
colour of darkness
the seismic chaos
of granite water
deathholds the land.

The Oystercatchers

for Molly and Louis Reid

The tide of the quiet heart
turns, and ebbs onto sand,
the oystercatchers circle in pairs,
the gannets fall straighter than any stone,
a light air flows over a plane of water, and

as quiet's the moment of place
at which all forces,
inward and out, the four elements
of living and dead, dance
on the needle of now,

so a light air ebbs down a cline of water,
the gannets have left their fishing,
the oystercatchers circle in pairs,   .
the tide of the quiet heart
turns, and flows against rock.

Three

for Robin Skelton

Between king and queen the joker calls
between river and tide the drowned man falls
between lover and lover a moment builds a wall

over lover and lover the long dark falls thick
over river and tide the gull wheels quick
over king and queen the joker bawls the trick

although king and queen are dead and gay
although lover and lover float in the bay
although river and tide carry them away

because river and tide clash in the bay
because lover and lover are night and day
because king and queen are stacked away

whenever river and tide run in one race
whenever king and queen overtake the ace
whenever this lover and lover come face to face

then will lover with lover refuse to play
then will king and queen obey, obey,
then will river and tide flow for a night and a day.

The Death and Birth of Simple Simon

Who is it knocking at the door
    so long before the light?
He must have come across the moor
    this black-as-Judas night.

Go down, go down, and let him in,
    whoever he may be;
tonight the devil should come in,
    for love, not charity.

Come in, come in, I'll light a light
    and start a fire as well;
before I crossed these fells tonight
    I'd burn content in Hell.

Come down, dear heart, come quick, come down;
    a child comes to be born.
I'll take the short way to the town;
    and be there by the morn.

Come down, sweetheart, come quick, come down,
    and ease your mother's pain;
the midwife's coming from the town
    through hail and wind and rain.

The child was born in the half light,
    was born and gave a cry:
the mother dead before the night,
    was dead without a sigh.

Come home, come home, my own dear love,
    you are too long away;
we have a child, by God above,
    who wed but yesterday.

Why wait, why knock upon the door?
    Come quick, dear love, come in!
But four men stood outside the door
    to carry her love in.

The sun shines bright upon the moor,
    although the wind is thin:
Fate knocks upon the outer door;
    Death on the door within.

Not That at All

She was not beautiful: it was not that at all.
She was not kind. Passionately she loved,
but none knew whom; perhaps she did not know.

Once in the street a funeral passed her by
and the stranger who was going to be buried
got up and begged her pardon for his death.

She was no witch: it was not that at all.

Descended into Hell

Terribly, a live one came among us dead.
His words were calm and comfortingly cold

but had—oh memory that makes bones sweat—
with them warm shadows, for they grew in light.

He did not jar us with a stepping tread:
but his still movement drew the wind inside

by which we burn, because its breath is live
and plays upon harmonics of our loves.

The Range of Night

No human word is absolute
in love; opaque, each word lets through

some greed of giving, lie of truth,
or virtue that corrupts the soul.

Silence alone is word enough
to speak of those the beast has mauled:

and yet by words they cairned the route
we take across the range of night.

Dream before Sleep

The day was blurring to dusk.
Lombardy poplars stood like privet under the wall.
I had reached this city on some other journey.

Between us and the gate we still saw through it
there stood, pyramid high—(yes, it was Egypt)—
a shadow carved in stone, the torso of a man,
his left side towards us, his head
a pattern of hollows, scooped out word by word
into a smoothness of bone, but still retaining
the coarse texture of its peeling scales,
for this was Yeats's beast still showing
—(a python's meal)—the shape of knowing man.

I watched this pallor of unmoving darkness breathe.
I noticed the wall extended for ever in all directions.
We were calm and quiet afraid, and did not fear
this Death we had made of words before the Nile.

Island of Clocks and Ghosts

The phoenix has been observed flying from the east of time,
    ice on his laughing wings,
        but no longer nests
here, where the fogs hunt down the twittering shadows of day

which already, it's thought, have learned to get down
    to the nesting ledges:
        at all events,
though observation is hard, some species of death has moved in.

Also, now the true birds have died out, the clocks have stopped ticking.
    There is, of course, no connection
        at all; simply
when silence struck midnight the clocks survived.

Poem of the Fancy

The first time I saw Death he was an old old man;
    nine hundred and sixty-nine they said, I think.

Next time I saw him there were red hairs among the grey;
    time makes its mark, they said.

When he taught us at school we showed him little respect,
    considering his decreasing years.

Last time I ran across him I noticed how much he'd unaged;
    he noticed me, too, and nodded.

His acquaintance, they say, turns in time to friendship;
    but that's as may be, I say.

I think that, after the usual formalities,
    young Death will quickly forget.

The Flutes

for Michael and Margaret Snow

The skull that shone its eyes of darkness on the dream
                    is Krakatoa high:
          I dance alone upon a cutting tooth,
while from the inmost corners of the speaking world
                    blow molten words
that still escape me though they drown us live.

An armoured shadow rose beneath the skull,
                    the eclipsing beast:
          I crawl alone upon a bridge of night,
while from the wheeling fells beyond the edge of time
                    the gusts of zero rise
that still elude me though they sink us home.

And swaddled in the absolute of dark,
                    the utter stop,
          I lie long dead among the abysmal ooze,
while from a nova on creation's eve
                    flutes strike our sight:
still their surrounding joy staves off skull, nothing, and the night.

Horn of a Dilemma

The trouble with unicorns,
useful as they were, and ornamental,
was their turning up on unsuitable occasions
and commenting pointedly
on eminent and important persons,
who appeared unflattered,
while ignoring unilaterally
learned and respectable persons,
who appeared unflattered.

The Uniqu'orn

The unicorn has changed his habits in cities, but whether
it's his special perception or his odd perversion's been lost
is a controversial subject, avoided
by the Commission appointed to consider the law
and the natural history, and make proper suggestions. It has,
however, consulted the lion, the poodle, the domestic ass, the cuckoo,
the gryphon and the praying mantis, and obtained some figures
about the rhino. The majority recommendations
are that the unicorn shall be confined to the parks
during daylight, and the horn painted invisible. The minority,
of course, put forward a number of viewpoints,
but agree that research is desirable
towards a companion for the present unique horn.
In view of the influence of Lady Ursula
and the Lord's Day Observance Society, a Government Bill
was expected, to limit unicorn hunting
to weekdays, but it's been left, in the end,
to a private member. Perhaps this is fitting.

St. George and the Dragon

for Tony Connor

Of the thousands who saw that sideshow a few
had resistant memories. One of these
told me before he died, keeping the soundtrack
in full cry, an oddly different story.

There was a notice, it seems, on the cage, saying:
'This dragon was captured
under the Economy, Dangers to, Order,
his natural food being bracken.
Feeding day Saturdays. Diet
prescribed by Caesar's physician. The girls
are all volunteers.' And what, to save an Economy
from the absence of rubbish, were a few girls
thrown to a dragon cub? There were always more,
and eager, too.

A good-natured pup, he would eat what he could,
so as not to insult the girls or disappoint the spectators,
but he often went hungry. Soon his breath
stank like an arterial road, and he lay,
his eyes like sad dimmed headlights,
staring at nothing, and gently howling for bracken.

Till one day he acted
in the most blasphemous way you can think of
towards a prelate of banking.

At the Festival they promised a foreign gent
a permit to stay in return for acting St. George,
but the great beast's breath put him right out.
The dragon was upset, too, and fanned him with awnings
until he came round. They parted good friends.
So the secular arm fell back on having him poisoned.

Who? Why, the dragon, of course.

In Passing

Yesterday, Aphrodite asked me the way,
and I, who was thinking about Happiness
and the Good Life, gave her most careful directions:
and am now a sigh in the wind, before snow.

Calvinist Funeral

We sat,
as their custom was,
round the boxed body;
and the minister of their sour religion
told God (for our ears)
what he thought fit.

And the true stern figure
lay there, helpless, at last, to rebuke
the hypocrite saved, and would never again
cheat, dear good woman, her wicked God
by smuggling a kindness through to the reprobate.

Silence is Truthful

In Memoriam Benjamin Brooke

'Words may be spoken though a voice is silent,
the wind rustle the leaves though they are absent,
and a thrush sing, yesterday, tomorrow.'

Silence is truthful; but these are words
whispered in the other ear at another time,
when evening has settled; today is night.

No one comes, and no one is awaited;
footsteps that come through the door are going away;
sleep may be dreamless: but a friend is dead.

Vanessa to Cadenus

If there are ghosts—aye, and if there are none—
I shall come, dying or dead, and live
certain past moments with you, and question
without fear or distorting words your heart,
and so you, time's needs being absent,
will find no hindrance from truth, no power
to hide pain, pity, contempt or love.

And when you have given your answer for good or ill
God may award his trivial heaven or hell.

The Quick Dead

Too many are dead: we can never mourn
with a mauve keening, with a tinkle of flowers, those
who with the gulls wheel, and the squadroned geese,
vulture, vampire (these too) and the farmyard fowl—
there was a flash—I saw him—green-blue up river—
redbreast, wren, and the rooks, with their rhyming slang.

There was—I see Blake, gentle with thunder,
'*In what rivers swim the sorrows, and upon what mountains
wave shadows of discontent, and in what houses . . .*',
and Kit Smart, drunk as a comet,
but God, and the Sombre Doctor, lead him home.
And in our minds the dull red candles smoke.

I, John Clare

I, John Clare, who have been many,
write now of my own self, John Clare
greatgrandson of John Clare, a family
of gardeners, parish clerks and fiddle players,
but eight greatgrandparents—suppose each father
in name was so in fact, but about that
how should I know, whose two wives are one,
and she, they tell me, dead, but I have seen her,
and why I am kept in this place I don't know.
Still, as I said (or Shakespeare, all the same),
all the world's a madhouse, though some
are friends—I think of Knight the steward,
who keeps and copies out for me my poems,
although he troubles me for missing lines
when many lines are missing from all lives.

When a small child I wandered out one day
across the summer heath until well lost
(and lost is sometimes well);
and there and back, to find the village seeking,
took me the whole long day
that's not yet done, though no one seeks me now,
for, having built walls round me, they suppose
I cannot wander now. But I go out
and find, as then, the farther flowers strange,
till my good lady comes to bring me home.

And went home once; the hedgerow winds
were bleak by night, but I reached home:
I saw home in the faces of some men, but did not know
the woman who, they told me, was my wife,
and so came, homeless, home

Courtship Dance

Note: the description of the redshank dance is based on that by Sir Julian Huxley in *Bird Watching and Bird Behaviour*.

Two small brown birds,
ordinary as ordinary words,
ordinary words.

See—he lifts his wings,
and they are pointed, white,
ha ha, white wings and scarlet shanks.

He steps out—right, left, right,
wings lifted, pointed, white.
He steps—but hear him sing
wild dancing gypsy song
of the redshank tongue,
heard far, heard long.

Look, his love listens, is watching,
perfectly silent, still.

He is going to her, right,
left, fanning his white
pointed wings, dancing
into the air his marching,
right, left, right,
white, scarlet, white,
lover towards his waiting silent love.

Suddenly he is there
and she away,
running, running,
leading the dance;
now she leads, he follows.

She runs, but not away;
she is circling, running;
at her first point, she stops.

And he? Look, he stops,
lifts his wings, pointed, white,
steps out with scarlet shanks,
begins his wild song, ha ha,
scarlet, white

This Adam saw. And he said—
God, make Eve.

Adam's Eve

*Suggested by a sculpture of a woman's head, found at Dolni
Vestonici. Its age is estimated at 20,000 or 25,000 years.*

for Robin Skelton

Adam's Adam

took rib of stone
took breath of word
took a beating star
took phoenix smoke

and made

with bone of his rock
with love of our savage heart
with gentle word of his poem
with eye of her daily sight

by his hand's love
by the pulse of those who are not yet born
by the words of those who had long been dead
by the sight of her ever eye

in colour beyond his eye
in time that has not yet circled the stars
in grief of delight
in the mind of God
in flesh and in blood

his Eve's Eve.

Epithalaminuet

for Hilary and John True

I wish you first what your own love will give, joy.
Next, to be happy. This your own sense will give you.
I wish you last what the Friendly Goddess gives
(O Most True, Most Friendly Goddess, Fortune!).

These wholly I wish you, and wish you also
to be fortunate in a time when it is not strange to be so.

By the authority committed unto you
I direct into Limbo

    the witchwomen with spells of blood,
    the witchmen with chains of words,
    the witchworms of gold and dead ages.

What, having had your wish, you would wish for, I wish you now.
What, having had, you would wish, that I wish you.

    I wish you a quiet lane
    with trees, and a west wind.

The Holy Places

for Rina

At the Place of Water
the tiger seeking his striped she
and the pygmy deer
awaiting his great-eyed dear
are at one. Here,
where all eyes are clean,
the dangerous shy goddess
throws the night sky from her
In the Place of Water.

At the Place of Air
to the dismay of priests,
for whom the plunging of Love
up up from the coupling seas
blasphemes Love hanged from the tree,
Lilith and the Archangel
of Day and the Dark clasp
their beating galactic wings
In the Place of Air.

At the Place of Earth
the tabby cat finding his striped she
and the buck rabbit
his goggling doe
have a single aim. Here,
where all words are plain,
the ambiguous frank mistress
wraps the daylight round her
In the Place of Earth.

At the Place of Fire—
Yes, indeed the phoenix:
that two-faced bird is us. And we
consume with troubling
over many things, with anger,
and what we are, and indeed
with love. For indeed Aphrodite
also was there and she blessed the wine
At Cana, in the Place of Fire.

A Deep Bright Crystal of Word

being a birthday poem for Margaret Snow

Three things were too hard
for King Solomon, yes four
he could not understand. The sun's fire
is locked in a crystal of water;
green columns of brown earth unfurl
gold crystals of Iris, flaunting
between here and for ever. Three
things, and four, the word and the paint
that make and are made, crystal as any mystery.
Three dimensions for making, and four
of all that is made. An ocean
of stillness bursts open a Word into Time
with perfection of three, an Iris, and for you
four seasons and winds of well.

Poem, if he had a Daughter

If our tune grows blurred,
idle, sudden, and day song,
if we think it absurd
after labouring all the light long
to dance all the dark third,

kiss us a dear word,
idle, sudden, and dusk song;
though we think it absurd
after labouring all the life long,
go, dance all the dark third.

When we hear no bird,
idle, sudden, and dawn song,
send us a light word
after labouring all the love long,
to dance in the dark world.

Dance, word.

Silver Poem for Rina

I

Crrrang!
The moon bursts into flower,
the river flows silver between black trees.
Crrang!

  But I am told that rather
  than paint the unicorns
  in the public gardens at Ramsgate,
  whose conduct was considered inappropriate,
  one should photograph the geraniums
  that so neatly portray the Lord Mayor.

Crrang! Crrrang!!

II

As we lay out in an open September night
near the Chesil Bank,
one swan with a flight certain as fate
was beating, beating, the resonant air.

Today we count
a reign of swans, one,
two, three . . . twenty-four, twenty-five.

III

Violets grew by the lane, blue and white,
primroses grew by the path, pale, tall,
moss was near them, and small bright shells
broken by a thrush, and gay
daffodils stood, in solemn thought.

The room was orange and blue.

Ferns, huge in a western wood, tiny on a northern wall,
cowslips on a southern cliff.
Mayflower, lines white across Hertfordshire.
Hedgesparrows' eggs, heavenblobs.
Kingcups, in a bowl with bluebells, and a few white.

The doors were scarlet, the walls cream.

After the bluebells and the beech
suddenly the wood was dark with larches.
Suddenly, again, the climbing path
was sunlit, sunshine on ling.
A young fox silently went in the bracken.

Golden willows, and silver, like fountains, played by the door.

The hill is steeper than those other hills.
The tempting route follows the white beck up
where red rowans shelter the pools,
but the true way goes up the spur.

The river brings a pair of swans to the door.

IV

Moon, daisies, quicksilver, night:
these are my love's.

If my love love not me
with joy, in peace, truly
darkness encircles me round.

Light.

The Unconceived

O
constellations of vacua, desert sands
empty of nothingness, well unspringing

and
o
daughters

O
deep-as-Adam snow, o million-magnified,
each uncrystal different as roses

and
o
sons

O
vast flights of souls, uncreated, swimming
on the plunging torrent of Lethe

and
o
daughters' sons

O
dark-year millions of no-one, unshaken spears
of ripe corn in infinite unploughed places

and
o
sons' daughters

O
numberless host inert at absolute zero
or travelling at light's pace into nothing
and
o

Oh, Ask, Ask

for those with child

Oh fish fish where are you swimming?
    In a secret sea.
Fish fish how may that be?
    Ask your thigh bone.

Oh bone bone where are you swimming?
    In a salt stream.
Bone bone how may that be?
    Ask your heart's tide.

Oh blood blood where are you swimming?
    In the Milky Way.
Blood blood how may that be?
    Ask your baby.

Oh baby my baby where are you swimming?
    In a fine house.
Baby my baby how may that be?
    Ask your great belly.

Oh belly belly you are a fine house
Oh baby my baby you are my love's joy
Oh blood blood Oh bone bone
Oh fish fish Oh song song
    You swim in my heart
      Oh heart heart

Statement at Christmas

As for his nature, which, how many, or how related,
        of this I know nothing.
Certainly as a man his nature is to be worshipped
and certainly a man's nature is never discarnate
        But in a market town
there was an explosion last night whose waves still surge
        after two thousand years
against the drums and trumpets of our inner shores
        silently.

As for substance and infinite and whence proceeding, of these too
        I am wholly ignorant.
Agreed whoever has the courage of his entire love
is a child raised to the power of God
        But at his heretic-stake
was lit the candle of whose flame all altars
        are flickering shadows,
was spoken the reverberant myth that echoes
        from faith to faith.

As for person, and the shamrock as image of God,
        I make no guess.
It is true that either Man is the image of God or God of Man
and there are three persons in one man
        But we celebrate
the bearing down of a child who is not yet born into time
        this night
from the 'great ring of pure and endless light'
        into the dark.

As for nature, substance, person, god and/or man, miraculous birth,
      I cannot say.
She bore him a normal time, and the birth
was as marvellous as yours or Spring's
      But the shuffle of words
was made, that deal, into a different pack
      for a gambling game
where love-all is method and stake and aim,
      the lawless, and only, rule.

And Because

'A star shines in the sky. He follows you. When you move he moves.'—Dictionary compiled by six-year-olds.

and because we listened

and listened not only among the incense and chanting
not only at premises of licensed amusement
not only in dreams or to the wisdom of actuaries

but listened also to the wind when we were lost in the mountains
listened in Petticoat Lane
or listened to silence and a heartbeat after the dawn

a word was spoken

and because we looked

and looked not only among the tinsel and holly
not only at neon bottles for Magog
not only at paper lanterns and the full moon

but looked over the sea to the west at sunset
looked also at the Auroral ballet
or looked at a glowworm and the light of word

a star shone in the sky

and because we walked

and walked not only along paved cloisters
not only to the holy cities of seven religions
not only by fieldpaths or Fleet Street

but walked also from Tolpuddle Hiroshima Sophiatown
walked awake and sleeping
or walked the King's Road as far as the Word's Beginning

the star came with us

and because the hotel was booked up for Christmas
we were boarded out with a girl who was nursing her baby

and the star stopped with us

and next day we continued our journey

Great St. Thomas Apostle

I have not departed. I am here to speak with God.
    I am not mad: my folly is not proud.
Since All is silent Nothing must speak the Word.

I will not leave Him be. I deny God.
    I am not mad: my folly is not proud.
I'll not affirm HE IS and, lying, damn my soul.

Though I lie dead I stand across His path.
    I am not mad: my folly is not proud.
Each death is a denial of His myth.

So speak, Great Judge, if You've a Word, or sentence,
    I shall attend with any ear You lend:
till then I'm in the box to prove the facts.

SILENCE IN COURT.

Canticle for the
Feast of S. Judas Iscariot

Daughter of Jesus, son of Satan, listen:

You were Nimrod: and you took flight from your shadow.

You were Ceres: and you sacrificed your children to the children of your shadow.

You were Orpheus: and you were the servant of the Cat.

You made yourself breasts of stone and arteries of water in the desert: and you worshipped Moloch.

You were Melchior; and with your gold you purchased monopolies of Caesar: Gaspar; and with frankincense you bought Herod: Balthazar; worshipper of Death.

You built cathedrals for God: and worshipped your shadow, saying: It has grown horns.

You were Dante: Minister of Propaganda.

You were Copernicus: and you have covered Venus with red flannel, lest the heavens should run amok.

You use the knife to save life: for you say: It can only kill one at a time.

You are Icarus: and you burrow in the ocean, seeking whom you may devour.

You have weighed the universe: and taxed the importation of knowledge.

You have freed the children: you have instructed them in the use of torture.

Daughter of Satan, son of Jesus, waken.

Father to the Man

I warned the parents, you know,
when he was a child. I said

This boy must really not be allowed
to argue about law with lawyers and about God
with theologians. And he seems, I said,
to fancy himself as a doctor, too. At this rate
we shall have him, perhaps, giving water
to a feverish patient. Little thinking
he'd do just that; and was lucky
the lad recovered.

It will come to no good, I said.
But one gets no thanks.

And so it went on
until, later, we lost touch;
for he was away for some years,
no one knew where.

Afterwards, I admit, I was half convinced. More than half,
I suppose I should say.

When he preached—and I shall hear no such sermons again—
it seemed that immutable right and wrong—
no, it was not that their boundaries changed. But somehow
acts and facts seemed with a shake of a word
to fall—I saw such a toy once, of foolish beads—
in a different pattern. What was done was the same,
and right and wrong were the same, and yet
not the same, being done in a different world.

There was a wedding, for instance,
with, in plain Aramaic, too much drink,
and you know the country customs—
I fear the old Gods are by no means dead.
Well, he was there, and he preached on the sabbath,
and spoke, just in passing, about the wedding;
and, you know, these junketings (to call them no worse)
seemed transformed, seemed a part
(like David's dancing in the Temple)
of our holy religion; and,
what is stranger, our religion
seemed to have grown, and to be our life.

Well, you see, it has come to no good,
as I told his parents, children
must listen, and lawful authority speak.

. . . and yet
        this is the saddest news . . . and I
        am nearer to death . . .

Some Word, Some Act, Some Footpath

for John White

I, who speak now, silent under the sun,
silent by moonlight, afraid by starlight,
hiding in forgotten corners, waiting
for God's dark mercy, I, brother to Judas,
speaking only when the dear dusk brings bats
with comfort from the tombs, I, who stowed
away in phantom ships, hoping
that some sea-god would have pity, I
who go in terror of kindness (for he was kind),
I, the wandering Jew, whom lepers shunned, the revenant
at whom the vampires shuddered, I who have sheltered
in the unlit corridors of madmen's brains,

I—oh, if you will but listen,
and, listening, believe, believing,
search in your memory what I forget . . .

There is some word, some act, some footpath,
known to the newborn child, as to the dead . . .

All else is nothing.

I lived, or some other, an ordinary man, loving
some two or three, and liking many,
suspicious of strangers, keeping,
within reason, the law, angry at small insults,
patient of wrongs, lived as my neighbours lived,
tired on Fridays, moderate in wine, I was never religious,
nor atheist either; when I died,
my widow, one might have thought, would have cried
a little, and remembered longer, not more than is decent,
and the neighbours
would have helped, being ordinary people,
that is to say, poor; and we had our customs,

And he, the herb doctor, known through Galilee,
having some power
a little uncanny, but a good man, gentle,
clever with a sick child, though too free
of God's name—that was before he
and a rabble crazy with religion, my brother one,
took to politics on street corners,
abusing the rulers, and the clergy, and defying the police.

Perhaps he, being unmarried, and a friend of the family,
and my wife—I thought once there would have been scandal
among prattling women; she young, and spoke so of him
after the boy next door, and he
never an observer of convention—

It would have been well, and I am sure,
with a sensible woman, still young,
he would have settled down, and studied his herbs,
and his other healings, nor my brother
meddled in politics, but died in bed,
and he, Joshua ben Joseph, have healed others,
not died young, and a bad death,
though, for him, quicker than was usual.

As for me, I was meant in nature
for good fortune in death. A little before,
the elders of the village had sent for me, saying,
Lazarus, you know
the table of the synagogue is old,
unworthy, and the chapel fittings
damaged in the commotions—meaning
when the rebels hid there, and the soldiers
would have wrecked the chapel, but a centurion
forbade it—and we know
that you are an upright man, and skilled, and one
who works for the glory of God,
and pays tithe, without hiding a profit,—
meaning, for I understood the cant,

You are honest, and take pride in your work,
and the village, and, for love of these things,
will do your best work, and charge no more
than the timber's cost,
and the charge to the rates will be little,
and the work good.

This, I say, I knew well enough, but, after all,
I was born and bred in that village,
and, by this work, I, an old man, should there be remembered;
and I took the job gladly,
and went to many synagogues, measuring,
with eye and with rule,
and waited a little, for good work
cannot be hurried, and travelled to Tyre
to buy the best wood. To cut a long story
short, on that day I had finished, and I knew
all the work good, agreeing each item with each,
and the table fit, almost, for Solomon's Temple, yet plain,
as befitted our village, and rightly proportioned
to the chapel, and its purposes, and no better table
in Galilee; I could do no better, nor any in Galilee.
There it stood, newly finished, and I
one moment looking with joy, and, the next,
dead. A good death, for which a man,
if he were religious, might pray.

Life is good, if one has reasonable luck,
as I had, and, after a good life, death.

After a good life, and one's best work finished,
death is good, if one has luck in its coming.

If you believe me, you may know, partly,
what then: my wife
strange, they said, with the shock of it, but she would have recovered—
she was always a sensible woman—
but, as fate would have it, he comes
three days after, and she distracted,

60

begging for a cure, as if I had the fever—
and he—what did he think? Was he crazy
even then, or not wishing to cross her?—
comes with her to the tomb, and prays, and God,
they said then, and, later, a devil,
and I cannot tell.

But I
came out
walking
from the tomb.

And they rejoiced then, but, after,
my wife feared, as I feared,
and he, after that, always among the mad sects,
and others forgot, for a time.

But I knew even then, both all and nothing,
for neither life remembered me nor death,
having done with me once.

And, at first, sat
silent in a corner, having forgotten
to live, and could not remember
to die, being
neither man nor ghost, but some other's body
containing the memory of my life, containing
these revolving thoughts, which in the dusk
I speak, if there is one to listen,
listening to believe and to remember,
to tell, but none tells me, nor you, either,
you will not tell.

He was a kind man, and a healer, and, I think, crazy,
for it was a cruel thing, and I an ordinary man,
not one to whom this
should have happened, and can find
no word. I think . . .

But there must
must be a word, or some act, or footpath . . .

some word which, spoken, some word
which, if I spoke,
I, the wanderer in darkness since they drove me,
fearing that they were born, and grew old, and I did not die,
they feared, and I, and cannot remember the act,
some word, some act, some footpath
into some life or death for me,
for me, brother to Judas, whom lepers shunned,
being neither man nor ghost, but a memory
forgotten by some God, forgotten by life and death,
I, the wanderer, silent under the sun,
silent by moonlight, afraid by starlight,
hiding in forgotten corners, waiting
for God's dark mercy. I, brother to Judas,
speaking only when the dear dusk brings bats
with comfort, a little comfort, from the tombs,
hiding in the unlit corridors of madmen's brains,

I—oh, if you have but listened,
and, listening, believed, believing

search in your memory what I forget.

Night Poem

THERE, in empty metaphysical Order,
where absolute zero liquidates the cold,
Here is proved Nowhere by timeless movement of clocks,
and Now disperses at a footrule's end.
Darkness shines in the dark: no poem is heard
above the silence of that infinite world.

HERE the galloping heart will shy
at a certain place, at a definite time.
Light shines in darkness. The candlelit sky
glistens, dew on a real web. For a line,
containing an image, was spoken by God
into the silence that still surrounds the Word.

Public Gallery

There are, we hear our voices say,
circumstances to extenuate
man's innocence, and aggravate
his laudable guilt. But facts and motives
are regrettably clear, attempted justice
compounded with the felony of love. Ancestors,
learned in conscience' law, answer,
reply, respond, rejoin, rebut,
pleading *in re God, ex parte Man*,
with surrebuttals and the rest for ever,
till you and Abel, Cain and I,
sworn, wigged, blackcapped, shaved for the rope,
go one by one away, the case not proved.

Come to Think of It

(for too many people to name)

I

Looking in the echo of light
cast on the green glass ball that stands
at the corner of the stairs, I find,
clearer than any fortune, events
that happen (and will) at some past time
when one comes to look in that direction.

II

Just as an echo in time is heard
at more than a point in space,
so an echo in space is seen
at more than a point in time.
I never saw, except in this glass ball,
this glass ball floating,
green glass in green water,
among green glass floats.

III

Still the wind increases: the floats and the net are gone.

IV

Light echoes light, across
the dark lapping river in a pattern of movement,
illumined moments or days rise and fall on the swirling years.
There is no ebb, and the time that flows
falls for ever, rising and falling, falling,
hurrying, avoiding the eye of the light,
that has no being until it is caught by a wave of time.

V

Corner of the stairs. Well, I shall turn again
in a nightmare or dream. In nightmare
there is no turning, and so a dream,
but I think waking. I remember
before memory a wolf howled at this place
a long way off, listening
(as I listen now) for another voice in his own
and perhaps (as with me now) she heard but could not retain,
but, waking or sleeping, I shall turn, and return

VI

and find, or be found. It is the poem
that writes, the man that is known by the thought,
and some place a long day from now
a God may turn on the stair, listening
for another voice in his own, and she
wolf to another? but the glass is silent, the river clouded,
the rulers are playing death against death,
and the stake is Death.

VII

The river is clear: the rulers are swept away.
The sea is clear, green as a float of memory. The hills
are ranges of stars. And perhaps
the God we have killed has risen again?
the glass has no word to say.

VIII

And the net of stars floats to an island beach.
Rain and seaspray and mist prepare them for brightness.

IX

Coming to look in some direction,
I see a dead Christ hanging upon His predestined cross.
Holiness weeps upon the hillside
and Aphrodite Antigone whispers a word to Joseph,
who gives his tomb to bury Man's body of love.

X

The green glass sparkles the tide of summer:
three friends cross the uncertain channel, find them, and bring them
    home;
and, scattered in inland England, they still reflect
the sea in the sun and collect such a day as this
(if you happen to look their day)
and make a thought between strangers.

XI

And those who love Him go quick
Is He risen indeed?
The glass has nothing to say—
the glasses float in the stormy bay,
out and away, they have nothing to say,
nothing to say.

XII

Whether or what man lived? is he living or dead?

A voice replies
In Time I know nothing, have nothing to say;
but the God rises, rises again:
this Church is His empty tomb.

Spare a Yesterday

What was that minim of flicker, that glottal stop
in the sentience of light? The young joys
have taken shelter, a memory has turned to leaf;
have taken shelter in shadow, has turned to a shadow of leaf.

Get out of here, enemy of the sun, the living are friends.
Get out of here, enemy of the moon, the dead are friends. Get out.

It's a day like this when I first remember the sun.
The day is for ever, the bushes are housetop high.
Gravely my father speaks of a centipede's legs
and tells me ground elder's the worst—I know it still—
of all weeds, and later I'm painted blue, the cure for a sting,
they decide, or should it be onion?—I still don't know.

But the shadow that fell on the book?
It was no shadow, and fell on no book,
not any shadow or book, not the starling's shadow
that flew above, nor the book upon which it fell.
Or not to matter.

For the phoenix casts no shadow,
for the swallow flying from dawn to dusk
is its own shadow, cast . . .
but there was no shadow. It was only a bubble of thought
that burst in the Gulf Stream, or Milky Way.

But today cast a shadow
those days.

And my father's mother
in the unbelievable town.
I remember one sun of day
they took me into a deep dark of house.

There were women, or women's shadows, in black, and one
had fingerstumps and a book of the gloom of God,
but the one I had come to see smiled by degrees, and said
words I forget, but light shines in the dark.

And let light shine.

Foxgloves grow to the sky.
I meet on a sun of day,
when a day is for ever,
my love, my first love. I remember her who
and her kiss, but do not remember 'who'
she was, or see her, I think, again.

Shadow casts light on the mind.

And an all-day flowing of sun.
My mother's father is ripe with rhymes
and full of intricate puns. I remember
a board and the magical pieces of chess.

But already the Black Queen
held him in check.

And I remember I learned of death
on a day like this, when the sun and the breeze
shone and blew in a Thomson poem,
and all was more bright about
the shadow that glanced against life,
night wrapped in an eyebright of time.

And they remembered.

And you have seen.

Did you notice a moment's shadow of blazing light
cast by the passing of all the dead?

Rest, rest.

Elegy for the Drowned

I

and especially a long-gone hour for the drowned

—once they were atlantic seal-lovers, combing
their Aphrodite-hair,
but we have so many instalments to pay
on the upholstered facts we have thought it best
to present the old myths to the museum
and dustbin the mythmaker: besides the saving of time
it comes cheaper to hire a myth from the morticians,
and they stock them in several very respectable patterns—

for the silence of the drowned cries out
above the fury of the water against the land

for here, since the sea drowned time from here to Scilly,
the silence of the drowned cries out
above the thump and swash of the eroding past
on the points and porths of being.

Oh batter down the breakers break the percussion
into component silence, the song of the dead.
Crash open the silence on rock, unfurl into flower
the tide's burst pods. Silence is speaking,
roaring into the mourners' hearts, the dead
that perhaps are mourning for us. Exquisite
the bad form with which they speak,
whether in silence or words.

the ebb is quiet, the ebbed are silent,
the nine-faced sea, that smothered them, mothers them now,
with her medusa-rollers she keens for her men,
mother and mistress of life she sobs or quietly weeps
for those she destroyed, with her careless claws
caresses all comers. But let's forget the drowner
and remember the drowned, from the beginning
and until the end, in an English churchyard

'. . . mariner, of Le Havre in France, the only son
of his mother, and she a widow'.

When the ebb is quiet the ebbed sleep quietly,

but when death
sucks the exhausted swimmer into his whistle,
charges up the river into the darkened town,
hurls the ship, brittle as a raw egg,
against the wall of the world,
the silence of the drowned accompanies
the sea's 'cello, the silence of the drowned
drowns the drums and trombones of the storm.

Rest, landsman and sailor, the only son
of your mother, and she a widow,
silence, and rest;

for only the restless antiphons of the sea
only silence among the candles of darkness

are dirge and requiem enough for the drowned.

Elegy Before Mourning

I

Some tide, perhaps, one of the dead,
who has cast no corpse, and is certainly not a ghost,
advances a short way back into life to find
—a sudden long wave against the ebb of the time—
one who in life is lost in the dead of alive,

but always to live or to die is to hear the sea
beat, to see the long time breakers toll
from never, to crash on now.

Certainly it's the dying
we must find breath to mourn,
dying confused with confusion of drug and pain
or dying quite still, calm as death, before death,
as I saw one die, gently (but is
the night good?—rest and light
for the living then), dying in terror or sleep,
and the fighting dead.

The sea pounds in the unmined veins;
the sea's crash and dirge are in us
and for us the out-tide's tow,

and in every lament and surge
the mourners are we who lie walking drowned
and drowned in the deep gulf and stream
under the choppy mind.

For candles—oh worth the poem—the twin pools, beginning to ice,
that were lit by laughter and burned love;
but the waters flow
for a difficult birth, labour uncertain and long
as the birth of a poem that presents the breech or is caught
in a stranglehold
of umbilical words; or perhaps dead quick.

II

If there is light it's human, and lives. And we must not leave
it to shadows to shine in the dark, lest we come to grief,

III

but must mourn now for the dying, for the dead
are deaf to endearment; with their great eyes
they see all nothing; for the skull's
the cast shell not the symbol of empty death.

Time ebbs into nothing. The dead
are those who will not be born. Time
flows out of nothing. The dying
are we who still mourn.

(Lazarus stepped from the foam
after a little death.)

And, going out, some have seen Fear
or The Sun, or some god. And some
—the inward sky lit,
in death's bright frost,
by galaxies of living and dead
and the tiderace of the unborn—
see all nothing
as the undertow drags out their lives
down a shingle of skulls, to the heaving dark.

IV

For the rest

best make light
of the dark,

yes, light.

The Voice

Wanders the proud sea-skimmer,
shambles the drowned

or so the voice said: but

we hide from time behind protective clocks:
their chimes assure us that the sun stands still

so the voice said: and

to speak a word one must listen listen
till perhaps perhaps one may one day be spoken a Word

and so the voice said: for

quiet roars into the heart
from the inmost knowledge of the night of ocean

so the voice says: and

74